1

TRUE
MASCULINITY

TRUE MASCULINITY

Become the Respected Man

DARRIN ELFORD

True Masculinity: Become the Respected Man

Copyright © 2025 by Darrin Elford

First published by Darrin Elford 2025

The information contained within this book is strictly for information and educational purposes only. If you wish to apply the ideas contained in this book, you are taking full responsibility for your actions.

ISBN: 978-1-991363-07-7 (Paperback)

eISBN: 978-1-991363-08-4 (E-Book)

First edition

Acknowledgements

Writing this book has been an incredible journey, and I'm deeply grateful to everyone who has played a part in making it possible.

First and foremost, I want to thank my family for their unwavering support and belief in me. Your love, patience, and encouragement have been my foundation. To my parents, thank you for teaching me the value of integrity, hard work, and respect—lessons that have shaped my understanding of what it means to be a man.

To my mentors and colleagues, thank you for challenging my thinking and pushing me to grow. Your insights and wisdom have been invaluable in shaping the ideas I've shared in this book. I owe so much to the conversations we've had and the lessons I've learned from you.

A special thank you to the readers who have trusted me with your time and attention. You are the reason this book exists. Your desire to learn and grow is the driving force behind every word written here. I hope that the ideas in these pages help you on your journey toward becoming the man you are meant to be.

To my team - editors, designers, and publishers - thank you for your hard work and dedication in bringing this project to life. Your professionalism and creativity have made this book something I'm proud to share with the world.

Lastly, I would like to thank every man who is on a journey of self-discovery and growth. Your commitment to becoming better leaders, better partners, and better versions of yourselves is what inspires me every day. This book is for you.

Thank you all for your support. I'm truly grateful.

Table of Contents

Introduction

Welcome to *True Masculinity: Become the Respected Man*. If you're holding this book in your hands, chances are you're feeling uncertain or confused about what it truly means to be a man in today's world. You've probably heard a lot about masculinity—on social media, in movies, or from friends—and maybe you're wondering which parts of it really matter. Perhaps you've felt pressure to fit into an image of what a man is supposed to be, but deep down, you know that version doesn't fully resonate with you. You may be tired of the surface-level portrayals of masculinity that don't speak to your real-life struggles, desires, or values.

This book is here to help you move from that confusion to a place of clarity and confidence. It's designed to take you on a journey—one that will help you discover and embrace your true, authentic self as a man. Along the way, you'll redefine masculinity in your own terms, breaking free from the stereotypes and pressures that have shaped your understanding of what it means to be a man.

The goal of this book is simple: to guide you in understanding and stepping into the kind of masculinity that is grounded in strength, integrity, authenticity, leadership, and respect—not the distorted version often shown in the media or expected by society. True masculinity isn't about being tough, cold, or emotionless. It's about being confident in who you are, standing firm in your values, and living a life of purpose and meaning. It's about leading with honor, connecting with others on a deeper level, and inspiring respect through your actions.

As you move through this book, you'll uncover the core principles that define true masculinity. You'll learn how to build confidence, manage your emotions, lead with authenticity, and earn respect not through force, but through integrity and character. By the end of this journey, you'll be able to stand tall as the man you're meant to be—strong, grounded, and deeply respected by those around you. Let's begin this journey together.

Modern Misconceptions of Masculinity

Modern Misconceptions

In today's world, when you think about what it means to be a man, chances are certain images or stereotypes come to mind. You might picture the "tough guy" who never shows weakness, or the "stoic" man who keeps his emotions locked away. Perhaps you think of a leader who is always dominant, always in control, and never lets his guard down. These images are all around us—through movies, social media, and even the way people talk about masculinity in everyday life. But here's the problem: these are just myths. They are not true representations of what it means to be a man. In fact, these distorted views can do more harm than good.

The first myth is the idea that a man must be tough—someone who never shows vulnerability, never admits to struggles, and always keeps up a facade of strength. We've all seen the portrayal of the "tough guy" in movies, in sports, and even in the workplace. This type of masculinity teaches us that being strong means not showing any weakness. But true strength is not about hiding emotions; it's about understanding and managing them. Hiding our emotions doesn't make us stronger—it makes us more disconnected from who we really are.

Then there's the idea of the "stoic" man—the one who is always calm and collected, never showing excitement or fear. This image tells men that they must be emotionally distant, never revealing what they truly feel. In reality, a man's ability to connect with his emotions is a key part of being emotionally intelligent and effective in relationships, both personal and professional.

Next, we have the myth of dominance. Society often suggests that a real man must be in control at all times—whether in relationships, work, or even social situations. Men are often expected to assert their power over others and to lead through force or aggression. But true masculinity isn't about dominating others. It's about leading with integrity, empowering others, and knowing when to step back and listen.

Finally, there's the idea that men must be emotionally distant. Society frequently encourages men to "tough it out" and "keep it together," pushing them to suppress their feelings and avoid expressing vulnerability. This emotional suppression leads to inner conflict. Men are taught to bottle up their emotions, and over time, this can lead to frustration, loneliness, and even mental health struggles.

These misconceptions are everywhere—on the big screen, in social media feeds, in advertisements, and even in the advice we hear from friends or family. They shape how we think about ourselves as men and how we believe we should behave in the world. But here's the reality: these myths don't reflect the true power of masculinity. They only show one narrow, distorted version of what it means to be a man.

The truth is, masculinity is not about being emotionless or always dominating others. True masculinity is about being authentic and embracing both strength and vulnerability. It's about being a leader who inspires through compassion, not force. It's about understanding your emotions and using them to build deeper connections with others. True masculinity is about living with integrity, leading with respect, and being in touch with your true self.

When you begin to let go of these myths and recognize them for what they are, you can start to understand what masculinity really means. The inner conflict and confusion you may feel will begin to fade as you embrace your true power, a power that comes from being confident in who you really are—not who society tells you to be.

In the next chapters, we'll dive deeper into what true masculinity really looks like and how you can step into it with confidence, authenticity, and respect. It's time to break free from the myths and embrace the man you were always meant to be.

Action Steps

In this chapter, we've explored the distorted versions of masculinity that are often portrayed in media and society—the tough guy, the stoic man, the dominant leader, and the emotionally distant individual. These myths are everywhere, but now it's time to take a step back and reflect on how these ideas may have shaped your beliefs, behaviors, and experiences. Understanding how these misconceptions have influenced you is the first step toward breaking free from them and embracing a more authentic, fulfilling version of masculinity.

Self Reflection – Your Misconceptions

How Have These Modern Views of Masculinity Influenced Your Beliefs and Behaviors?

Take a moment to think about the messages you've received about what it means to be a man. These messages might have come from movies, TV shows, friends, family, or social media. The media often glorifies the "tough guy" who doesn't show emotion, the stoic man who never appears vulnerable, or the dominant leader who is always in control. These portrayals are powerful, but they don't represent the full picture of masculinity.

Ask yourself these questions:

- **What images of masculinity did I grow up with?**

Did you see men as figures of authority and control? Were emotions seen as weaknesses?

- **How have these ideas influenced the way I act?**

Do you suppress your emotions because you fear appearing weak? Are you more focused on being dominant rather than genuinely connecting with others?

- **How do I feel when I try to fit into these roles?**

Do you ever feel like you're not being true to yourself when you try to meet these expectations? Is there a part of you that feels disconnected or exhausted from living up to these images?

The answers to these questions can help you identify how deeply these myths have influenced your perception of yourself and the way you engage with the world.

1. Identify the Areas Where These Misconceptions Have Led to Confusion or Dissatisfaction in Your Life

Once you've reflected on how these societal views have shaped your thinking, it's time to look at how they might have caused confusion or dissatisfaction in your life. These misconceptions often lead men to feel like they're failing to meet impossible standards, or that they are somehow less of a man because they don't fit the mold.

Consider the following:

- **In your relationships:**

Have you ever held back emotions or avoided vulnerability because you were taught that "real men don't cry" or "you have to be strong all the time"? Has this created distance between you and those you care about?

- **In your work life:**

Do you feel pressure to always be the leader, to take charge, or to assert control—even when it doesn't feel natural to you? Have you ever avoided asking for help or sharing your struggles because you didn't want to appear weak?

- **In your personal growth:**

  Do you feel stuck or confused because you're constantly trying to be someone you're not? Do you find yourself exhausted by the constant effort to keep up appearances or meet societal expectations?

As you reflect, take note of areas in your life where you've felt frustrated or disconnected. These are often the places where the myths of masculinity have caused confusion or dissatisfaction. The pressure to fit into a version of masculinity that doesn't align with who you truly are can lead to feelings of inadequacy, loneliness, and burnout.

2. Start Breaking Free from the Myths

Now that you've reflected on how these misconceptions have influenced your life, it's time to take the first step in breaking free. Acknowledging these influences is powerful because it allows you to make a conscious decision to redefine masculinity on your own terms. You don't have to fit into the narrow, outdated images that society often pushes.

Here are a few ways to start:

- **Embrace vulnerability:**

  Recognize that being open and honest about your feelings is a sign of strength, not weakness. Whether it's in your personal relationships or at work, allowing yourself to be vulnerable can deepen your connections with others and improve your emotional well-being.

- **Challenge the need for dominance:**

  Leadership isn't about being in control all the time. It's about inspiring others, listening with empathy, and guiding with integrity. Shift your focus from "how can I dominate?" to "how can I lead with respect and compassion?"

- **Redefine strength:**

    True strength comes from within. It's about having the courage to be authentic, to stand up for what you believe in, and to take responsibility for your actions. Strength isn't about being unbreakable; it's about being resilient and adaptable in the face of life's challenges.

3. Action Step: Create Your Own Definition of Masculinity

Now, I encourage you to create your own definition of masculinity—one that is true to who you are, rather than what society or the media tells you it should be. Think about the qualities you admire in men who inspire you. Maybe it's a father, a mentor, or a public figure who exemplifies the type of masculinity you aspire to. Consider the following questions:

- **What values are most important to me as a man?**

    Think about integrity, respect, authenticity, responsibility, and empathy.

- **What does being a "strong" man really mean to me?**

    Strength can look different for everyone. For some, it might be physical; for others, it could be emotional or intellectual.

- **What kind of man do I want to be in relationships, work, and life?**

    Think about how you want to show up in the world—honest, compassionate, confident, or grounded.

By identifying these core values and qualities, you begin to move away from the misconceptions and step into the power of being your true self.

These actionable insights are the first steps on your journey to understanding and embracing true masculinity. As you begin to recognize how the myths of masculinity have influenced you, you'll feel a sense of clarity and freedom that comes with letting go of the societal expectations that no longer serve you. This is your path to becoming the respected man you are meant to be.

2

Core Principles of True Masculinity

The Principles of True Masculinity

In this chapter, we'll dive into the foundational principles that make up true masculinity. These are the qualities that allow you to stand confidently as a man, fully aware of who you are and what you stand for. They are the keys to becoming the type of man who is not only respected but also at peace with himself. By embracing these principles—self-awareness, integrity, authenticity, emotional intelligence, and leadership—you will begin to step into your true masculine power.

Self-Awareness: The Importance of Knowing Who You Are and What You Stand For

Self-awareness is the cornerstone of true masculinity. It's about understanding yourself deeply—your values, your strengths, your weaknesses, and your beliefs. Without self-awareness, it's easy to be swayed by external influences or to live a life based on the expectations of others. But when you are self-aware, you know exactly who you are, what you believe in, and what you stand for.

Being self-aware allows you to live with purpose. It means you can make decisions that are aligned with your values, not because someone else told you to, but because they reflect who you truly are. Self-awareness also gives you the clarity to set goals and pursue them with confidence, knowing that the path you're walking is your own.

Ask yourself these questions:

- What are my core values?
- What are the things I care most about in life?
- What do I want to stand for as a man?

The answers to these questions will help you navigate life's challenges with a strong sense of direction. When you are in tune with yourself, you won't get lost in the noise of societal expectations or peer pressure.

Integrity: Living in Alignment with Your Values, No Matter the Circumstances

Integrity is the practice of living in alignment with your core values and beliefs, no matter what the situation is. It means doing the right thing, even when no one is watching, and standing firm in your convictions, regardless of external pressures.

True masculinity isn't about pretending to be perfect or always following the crowd—it's about being true to yourself and acting in ways that reflect your values. When you live with integrity, you earn respect from others, not because you demand it, but because your actions consistently reflect honesty, responsibility, and commitment to your principles.

Consider these questions to assess your integrity:

- Do my actions align with my beliefs and values?
- When faced with tough decisions, do I choose what's right over what's easy?
- Am I honest with myself and others, even when it's uncomfortable?

Living with integrity is powerful because it builds trust—trust in yourself and trust from others. It allows you to walk through the world with confidence, knowing that you are living authentically and consistently.

Authenticity: Being Comfortable with Your True Self and Not Trying to Fit a Mold

Authenticity is the ability to be yourself, unapologetically. It means not trying to fit into the narrow definitions of masculinity that society often imposes. True masculinity isn't about living up to a particular image or expectation—it's about embracing your individuality and being comfortable with who you are.

The pressure to conform can be overwhelming, especially with the influence of social media and societal standards. But trying to fit into someone else's idea of who you should be only leads to frustration and self-doubt. When you accept and express your true self, you open the door to genuine happiness and fulfilment. You stop pretending, and you start living.

Ask yourself these reflective questions:

- Do I feel comfortable in my own skin, or am I constantly trying to be someone I'm not?
- Am I afraid of being judged for showing who I really am?
- What parts of myself have I hidden or suppressed to fit in?

Being authentic isn't always easy. It requires courage to let go of the mask you've been wearing and embrace the person you are underneath. But once you start living authentically, you'll feel more at peace and more in control of your life. Authenticity builds deeper connections with others because it invites them to be real with you, too.

Emotional Intelligence: Understanding and Managing Your Emotions to Enhance Relationships and Decision-Making

Emotional intelligence (EQ) is the ability to understand, manage, and express your emotions in healthy ways. It also involves recognizing and responding to the emotions of others. Contrary to the myth that men should be emotionally distant, emotional intelligence is an essential part of true masculinity.

When you are emotionally intelligent, you can manage stress, handle conflicts better, and communicate more effectively. EQ helps you build stronger, more meaningful relationships—whether at work, in friendships, or in intimate partnerships. It's about understanding that your emotions are a powerful tool for connection, not a weakness to be hidden.

Here's how you can develop emotional intelligence:

- **Self-awareness:**

  Start by recognizing your emotions as they arise. Are you feeling angry, anxious, or frustrated? Understanding your feelings helps you respond to them constructively.

- **Self-regulation:**

  Learn to control impulsive reactions. Instead of lashing out when upset, take a step back and assess the situation before responding.

- **Empathy:**

  Try to understand the emotions of others. What are they feeling, and how can you support them? Emotional intelligence isn't just about managing your own emotions—it's about connecting with others on a deeper level.

The more you develop your emotional intelligence, the better equipped you'll be to handle life's ups and downs with grace and maturity. EQ allows you to lead by example and create environments where others feel valued and understood.

Leadership: The Power of Leading by Example and Inspiring Respect Through Your Actions, Not Your Words

True leadership is about leading by example. It's not about barking orders or asserting dominance—it's about inspiring others to be their best selves by demonstrating the qualities you want to see in the world. When you live with integrity, authenticity, and emotional intelligence, you naturally become a leader others respect.

Leadership is earned through actions, not words. It's about being consistent in what you say and what you do. When you show up as a man who embodies these principles, others will naturally look to you for guidance and inspiration. Leadership is about serving others and lifting them up, not about proving you're the most powerful person in the room.

Consider these leadership qualities:

- **Lead with empathy:** Understand the challenges others face and offer support when needed.
- **Be accountable:** Own your mistakes and learn from them.
- **Be a role model:** Demonstrate the values and behaviors you want others to follow.

True leaders don't seek power for their own gain—they seek to empower those around them, creating an environment of trust and respect. When you lead by example, you inspire others to follow in your footsteps.

Conclusion

The core principles of true masculinity—self-awareness, integrity, authenticity, emotional intelligence, and leadership—are the foundation for a strong, confident man who is respected by others. These qualities allow you to live with purpose, make decisions that align with your values, and lead with integrity. By embracing these principles, you can step into the powerful, authentic version of yourself that not only commands respect but also brings fulfilment and happiness.

As you continue on this journey, remember that true masculinity is not about conforming to an image; it's about discovering and becoming the best version of yourself. When you live by these principles, you'll be on the path to becoming the respected man you were always meant to be.

Self Reflection – Chapter 2

Now that we've discussed the key principles of true masculinity—self-awareness, integrity, authenticity, emotional intelligence, and leadership—it's time to put these ideas into practice. In this section, we'll focus on actionable exercises and reflection questions that will help you identify your core values, passions, and strengths, explore your true self, and challenge societal norms. These tools are designed to help you align your life with the principles of true masculinity and begin to make real changes.

1. Exercise: Identifying Your Core Values, Passions, and Strengths

To become the man you are meant to be, it's important to first understand what truly matters to you. Your core values are the beliefs and principles that guide your decisions, behavior, and interactions with others. Your passions are the things that light you up and give you a sense of purpose. And your strengths are the talents and skills you naturally excel at—these are the areas where you can make the most impact.

Here's a simple exercise to help you identify these aspects of yourself:

Step 1: Identify Your Core Values

Think about the things that are most important to you. What do you stand for? What do you want to be known for? Some common core values include honesty, loyalty, respect, kindness, and courage. Write down at least 5-10 core values that resonate with you. If you're unsure, ask yourself questions like:

- What do I want to stand up for in my life?
- What makes me feel proud of myself?
- What kind of man do I want to be?

Step 2: Discover Your Passions

Next, think about what excites you—what activities, causes, or interests make you feel alive and energized? Write down the things that bring you joy, fulfillment, and purpose. Don't worry about what others might think—this is about what truly lights you up. Ask yourself:

- What activities make me lose track of time?
- What would I do if money and time weren't an issue?
- What makes me feel most connected to myself and others?

Step 3: Identify Your Strengths

Your strengths are the skills, talents, and qualities you possess that come naturally to you or that you've developed over time. These are areas where you can excel and offer value to others. To discover your strengths, think about the tasks or activities where you've had the most success.

Consider:

- What do others often compliment me on?
- What do I feel most confident doing?
- When have I received positive feedback for my actions?

Once you've completed these steps, you'll have a clearer sense of your core values, passions, and strengths. These are the guiding principles that will help you live a life of authenticity and integrity.

2. Reflection Questions: Explore Your True Self and Challenge Societal Norms

Now that you've identified your core values, passions, and strengths, it's time to reflect on how these qualities align with the version of masculinity you've been taught by society. Often, societal norms encourage men to fit into a narrow box—one that doesn't always allow room for authenticity or emotional expression.

Use these reflection questions to explore your true self and challenge the societal expectations that may no longer serve you:

- **What are the expectations I feel society places on me as a man?**

  Write down the messages you've received about what it means to be a man. These might include ideas about how men should act, what they should value, or how they should look.

- **How do these societal expectations make me feel?**

  Do they make you feel confident, or do they create pressure, confusion, or frustration? Are you trying to fit into a mold that doesn't feel authentic?

- **In what areas of my life am I pretending to be something I'm not to fit in?**

  This could be in your career, relationships, or social life. Reflect on how you might be hiding your true self in order to meet external expectations.

- **What parts of me have I suppressed or ignored because they don't align with society's view of masculinity?**

Maybe you've suppressed your emotions, avoided vulnerability, or neglected your passions to fit into a "manly" image. What would it look like if you embraced these parts of yourself instead?

Challenging societal norms is about breaking free from the expectations that don't align with your authentic self. It's about creating space for a masculinity that is rooted in who you truly are, not in what others tell you to be.

3. Real-Life Examples of Men Who Embody True Masculinity

To help you visualize what true masculinity looks like in action, let's explore a few real-life examples of men who embody the core principles we've discussed: self-awareness, integrity, authenticity, emotional intelligence, and leadership. These men show us that masculinity can take many forms, and the power of true masculinity lies in embracing who you are, not in conforming to a rigid ideal.

Example 1: Nelson Mandela

Nelson Mandela is a powerful example of true masculinity. He was a man who stood firm in his values—justice, equality, and peace—even when it meant sacrificing his own freedom for decades. His integrity and commitment to his principles earned him the respect of the world. Mandela was also emotionally intelligent, understanding the importance of empathy and forgiveness in healing a divided nation. He led by example, showing that true leadership is about serving others and acting with courage and compassion.

What We Can Learn:

True masculinity isn't about dominance or control—it's about standing firm in your beliefs and leading with empathy and compassion.

Example 2: Dwayne "The Rock" Johnson

Dwayne Johnson, known as "The Rock," is a modern example of a man who embraces his authenticity. While he is known for his physical strength, he's also an advocate for mental health, often sharing his personal struggles with anxiety and depression. Johnson's transparency about his emotions and willingness to be vulnerable have made him a role model for many men who might otherwise feel pressured to hide their struggles. He's not afraid to show that being a strong man includes caring for your mental and emotional well-being.

What We Can Learn:

True masculinity means being comfortable with who you are—strength doesn't come from hiding your emotions, but from being open and vulnerable when needed.

Example 3: Barack Obama

Barack Obama is another man who embodies true masculinity. As a leader, he demonstrated self-awareness, emotional intelligence, and integrity. He showed us that leadership doesn't require aggression or dominance—it requires clarity of vision, a commitment to values, and the ability to listen and empathize with others. Obama's leadership was grounded in respect and authenticity, which earned him the admiration of people from all walks of life.

What We Can Learn:

Leadership is about leading with respect and empathy, not through force or intimidation. True masculinity includes listening, learning, and uplifting others.

Conclusion

These exercises and real-life examples provide a blueprint for how you can begin to step into your true masculinity. By identifying your core values, passions, and strengths, challenging societal norms, and learning from men who embody these principles, you can start building a life that aligns with who you truly are. True masculinity isn't about fitting into a predefined mold - it's about embracing your authentic self, leading with integrity, and building meaningful connections with others. Start today, and watch as you grow into the man you're meant to be.

3

Challenges to Authentic Masculinity

Overcoming the Challenges to Masculinity

We'll explore the internal barriers that often prevent men from fully embracing their true masculinity. These barriers include the fear of judgment and rejection by others, the internal conflicts that arise when we try to express emotions and vulnerability, and the self-doubt and negative self-talk that can undermine our confidence. The journey to authentic masculinity is not without its challenges, but overcoming these obstacles is what leads to true strength, resilience, and fulfilment.

The Fear of Judgment and Rejection by Others

One of the greatest fears men face when embracing true masculinity is the fear of being judged or rejected by others. Society has constructed a very specific image of what it means to be a "man"—strong, stoic, and unemotional. When we stray from these expectations, we risk being seen as weak or less-than. This fear of judgment can be paralyzing, and it often holds us back from living authentically.

It's important to recognize that this fear is rooted in societal conditioning, not in truth. The pressure to conform is intense, especially in a world that often praises superficial displays of strength or power. However, true masculinity is not about meeting the standards set by others—it's about being true to yourself, regardless of what others think.

To begin overcoming the fear of judgment, ask yourself:

- Whose approval am I seeking? Is it truly important for me to meet their expectations?
- What would it look like if I chose to live authentically, without fear of judgment?

- How can I accept and appreciate the fact that not everyone will understand or approve of my choices?

Remember, the fear of rejection is natural, but it's also something that can be overcome. The more you practice embracing your true self, the less power this fear will have over you. True respect comes not from conforming to external expectations, but from standing firm in who you are, regardless of others' opinions.

Overcoming Internal Conflicts: Embracing Emotions and Vulnerability

Another significant challenge men face in embracing their true masculinity is the internal conflict around expressing emotions and vulnerability. Many men have been taught that showing emotions is a sign of weakness, that "real men" don't cry, don't show fear, or don't expose their vulnerabilities. As a result, men often bury their emotions and put up walls, thinking that they must appear tough at all times.

The truth is, emotions are not a sign of weakness—they are a natural part of being human. Vulnerability, when expressed healthily, is a powerful way to connect with others and to grow. It takes courage to show vulnerability, but doing so allows you to live more authentically and deeply. Embracing your emotions doesn't make you less of a man; it makes you a more complete and powerful one.

To begin overcoming these internal conflicts, try these steps:

- **Acknowledge your emotions:**

    Start by identifying what you're feeling. Are you angry, sad, anxious, or frustrated? Don't judge yourself for having these emotions—just recognize them.

- **Express your feelings:**

Find healthy ways to express your emotions, whether that's talking with a trusted friend, writing in a journal, or even simply sitting with your feelings in silence. It's important to give yourself the space to process your emotions without judgment.

- **Challenge your beliefs:**

    Reflect on the beliefs you've been taught about masculinity and vulnerability. Are these beliefs serving you? Are they based on truth, or are they limiting you from being fully yourself?

The more you allow yourself to feel and express emotions, the more you'll find that vulnerability is actually a source of strength, not weakness. True masculinity includes the ability to be in touch with your emotions and express them in ways that build connection, trust, and authenticity.

Confronting Self-Doubt and Negative Self-Talk

Self-doubt and negative self-talk are powerful forces that can undermine your confidence and sense of self-worth. Many men experience these thoughts, especially when trying to break free from societal expectations or when embracing vulnerability. It's easy to question your worth, especially when you're stepping outside of the mold that others expect you to fit into.

The key to overcoming self-doubt is understanding that these thoughts are not facts—they are simply beliefs that we've learned to accept over time. You have the power to challenge and reframe these negative thoughts. By shifting your perspective, you can build your self-confidence and develop a more positive, empowering mindset.

Here are some strategies for confronting self-doubt and negative self-talk:

- **Recognize the thought patterns:**

  Pay attention to the negative thoughts you have about yourself. Do you tell yourself you're not good enough, not strong enough, or not worthy of respect? Recognizing these thoughts is the first step in changing them.

- **Challenge the beliefs:**

  Ask yourself if these negative beliefs are true. Where did they come from? Are they based on your own experiences, or are they societal messages that you've internalized? Often, these beliefs are not based in reality but are shaped by external expectations or past experiences.

- **Replace negative self-talk with positive affirmations:**

  Instead of telling yourself that you're not enough, practice affirming your strengths, values, and qualities. Remind yourself that you are worthy, capable, and powerful, just as you are.

- **Focus on your progress, not perfection:**

  Growth is a process, and setbacks are part of that journey. Instead of criticizing yourself for mistakes, focus on the progress you've made and the lessons you've learned along the way.

When you confront self-doubt and replace it with positive affirmations, you'll gradually build a stronger, more resilient sense of self. Remember, confidence is not about being perfect—it's about believing in your own ability to grow, learn, and rise above challenges.

Building Resilience: Embracing Challenges and Criticism

Life will inevitably present challenges and criticism, especially when you choose to live authentically. You may face opposition from others, or even from within yourself. The path to true masculinity is not always easy, but resilience—the ability to bounce back from setbacks and keep moving forward—is a key part of building strength and confidence.

Building resilience begins with accepting that challenges and criticism are part of life. Instead of viewing them as obstacles, see them as opportunities for growth. Each challenge you face is a chance to learn more about yourself and to develop the mental and emotional strength to overcome adversity.

Here are a few tips for building resilience:

- **Embrace discomfort:**

  True growth happens outside of your comfort zone. When you push through discomfort and adversity, you become stronger and more capable. Don't shy away from challenges—embrace them as opportunities to grow.

- **Learn from criticism:**

  Criticism can be difficult to hear, but it can also be a valuable tool for improvement. Instead of reacting defensively, try to see the feedback as an opportunity to learn. Is there any truth in the criticism? How can you use it to become a better version of yourself?

- **Cultivate a growth mindset:**

  Instead of focusing on failure, focus on progress. A growth mindset allows you to see mistakes as stepping stones toward success. Keep moving forward, even when things don't go as planned.

Remember, resilience isn't about avoiding failure or discomfort—it's about persevering through it. With time, you'll develop the mental toughness to handle whatever challenges come your way, and you'll become even stronger as a result.

Conclusion

The journey to embracing your true masculinity is not without its challenges, but it's in overcoming fear, doubt, and vulnerability that you'll find your true strength. By confronting the fear of judgment, embracing your emotions, challenging self-doubt, and building resilience, you will step into a life of authenticity and power. True masculinity is not about conforming to societal norms or hiding your true self—it's about living in alignment with your values, showing vulnerability, and embracing challenges with courage and resilience. As you continue on this path, remember that every obstacle is an opportunity to grow, and the man you are becoming is one who is stronger, more confident, and more respected than ever before.

Self Reflection – Chapter 3

Now that we've explored the challenges that prevent many men from embracing their true masculinity—such as fear of judgment, internal conflicts, self-doubt, and vulnerability—it's time to put some practical strategies into action. The goal of this section is to provide you with concrete exercises and techniques that will help you confront limiting beliefs, build emotional resilience, and embrace vulnerability as a source of strength.

1. Practical Exercises to Confront and Challenge Limiting Beliefs About Masculinity

Many of the beliefs we hold about masculinity are shaped by society and past experiences, not by our authentic selves. These limiting beliefs can hold you back from living fully and confidently as the man you are meant to be. To break free from these beliefs, it's important to identify them, challenge them, and replace them with more empowering perspectives.

Here's a simple exercise to help you do just that:

Step 1: Identify Your Limiting Beliefs

Start by reflecting on the messages you've received about masculinity throughout your life. These messages may have come from family, friends, media, or society. Write down any beliefs or assumptions you hold about what it means to be a "real man." Some examples might include:

- "Men don't show weakness."
- "I need to be tough and stoic all the time."
- "Real men don't cry."
- "I must always be in control."

Step 2: Challenge Your Beliefs

Now, for each limiting belief you've written down, ask yourself the following questions:

- Is this belief based on my own values and experiences, or is it something I've been taught by others?
- Is this belief serving me or holding me back from living authentically?
- What would happen if I let go of this belief? How would my life improve if I embraced a different, more empowering perspective?

Step 3: Replace with Empowering Beliefs

Once you've challenged these limiting beliefs, replace them with more empowering, authentic beliefs. For example:

- "True strength comes from being vulnerable and expressing my emotions."
- "I can show leadership and power without sacrificing my authenticity."
- "It's okay to seek support and ask for help when needed."

By identifying and challenging these limiting beliefs, you'll begin to free yourself from the societal pressures that have shaped your view of masculinity. Replacing these beliefs with more empowering ones will allow you to live with greater authenticity and confidence.

2. Techniques for Building Emotional Resilience and Managing Fear

Building emotional resilience is crucial for navigating the inevitable challenges and setbacks you'll face on your journey to true masculinity. Emotional resilience means being able to face adversity, criticism, and fear without allowing them to break you down. It's about having the inner strength to bounce back, learn from difficult experiences, and continue moving forward.

Here are a few techniques you can use to build emotional resilience:

Technique 1: Practice Mindfulness and Self-Awareness

Mindfulness is the practice of being present and aware of your thoughts, feelings, and physical sensations without judgment. It allows you to observe your emotions rather than react impulsively. Practicing mindfulness can help you manage fear and stress by allowing you to stay calm and centered in the face of challenges.

How to practice:

- Take a few minutes each day to sit quietly and focus on your breath.
- Notice any emotions or thoughts that arise, but don't judge them or try to change them. Simply acknowledge them and let them pass.
- If you feel fear or anxiety, acknowledge it without letting it control you. Focus on your breath and remind yourself that emotions are temporary and don't define you.

Technique 2: Reframe Negative Thoughts

When fear or self-doubt arise, it's easy to fall into negative thinking patterns. Reframing these thoughts can help you shift your perspective and build emotional resilience.

How to reframe:

- When you catch yourself thinking "I'm not good enough," ask yourself, "What evidence do I have that this is true?"
- Replace the negative thought with a more positive, empowering one, such as "I am capable of growing and improving every day."
- Focus on your strengths and past successes. Remind yourself of times when you overcame fear or adversity before.

Technique 3: Build a Support System

Emotional resilience doesn't mean facing challenges alone. Surround yourself with supportive people who encourage your growth and remind you of your strengths. This support system can include friends, family, mentors, or even a therapist or counselor. Having people who believe in you will help you stay resilient during tough times.

3. Strategies for Embracing Vulnerability as a Source of Strength

Vulnerability is often seen as a weakness in traditional views of masculinity. However, true masculinity is rooted in embracing vulnerability as a source of power and connection. When you allow yourself to be vulnerable, you show courage, authenticity, and emotional depth. Vulnerability builds trust in relationships and allows you to connect with others on a deeper level.

Here are some strategies for embracing vulnerability as a strength:

Strategy 1: Start Small and Practice Vulnerability Gradually

If you've spent a long time suppressing vulnerability, it might feel uncomfortable at first. Start by practicing small acts of vulnerability and gradually build up to bigger ones. This might include expressing your feelings to someone close to you, admitting when you don't know something, or asking for help when you need it.

How to practice:

- Share something personal with a trusted friend or partner. This could be a fear you've been holding onto, a mistake you've made, or a feeling you're struggling with.
- Don't worry about having the perfect words—vulnerability is about honesty, not perfection. Speak from the heart and allow yourself to be open.

Strategy 2: Reframe Vulnerability as Courage

Instead of seeing vulnerability as a weakness, start viewing it as an act of courage. Being open and honest about your emotions requires bravery, especially in a world that often encourages men to hide their feelings.

Reframing vulnerability in this way will help you see it as a strength rather than something to be feared.

How to reframe:

- Remind yourself that every time you allow yourself to be vulnerable, you are showing strength by embracing your true self.
- Consider the times in your life when vulnerability led to deeper connections, greater understanding, or personal growth. These moments are evidence of the power that vulnerability holds.

Strategy 3: Cultivate Self-Compassion

Being vulnerable means allowing yourself to be imperfect. It's essential to practice self-compassion, especially when you feel exposed or vulnerable. Treat yourself with the same kindness and understanding that you would offer a close friend who is going through a difficult time. When you embrace self-compassion, you allow yourself the space to be imperfect without judgment.

How to practice:

- When you feel vulnerable or make a mistake, instead of criticizing yourself, speak to yourself with kindness: "It's okay to be human. I'm learning and growing."
- Accept that being vulnerable doesn't make you less of a man—it makes you more human, more connected, and more authentic.

Conclusion

By using these actionable insights, you can begin to break free from limiting beliefs about masculinity, build emotional resilience, and embrace vulnerability as a source of strength. The path to true masculinity is not about conforming to societal expectations—it's about being honest with yourself, accepting your emotions, and having the courage to be vulnerable. As you practice these strategies, you'll grow stronger, more confident, and more aligned with your true self. Remember, vulnerability is not a weakness—it's a power that will enable you to live with greater authenticity, connection, and strength.

4

The True Power of Masculinity

Authentic Living as a Respected Man

In this final chapter, we'll explore the transformative power of living authentically and confidently in every area of your life. From personal relationships to your role in the workplace and social circles, embracing your true masculinity leads to deeper connections, greater influence, and lasting respect. You will also discover the importance of continuous self-improvement, how to build meaningful relationships rooted in mutual respect, and how your actions as a leader can leave a legacy that shapes the world around you.

The Power of Living Authentically in All Areas of Life

When you embrace your true masculinity, you are no longer playing a role or pretending to be someone you're not. Living authentically means being true to your values, your emotions, and your passions in all aspects of life. This authenticity has a powerful impact on your relationships, work, and leadership.

In personal relationships, when you live authentically, people are drawn to you. They respect you because you are consistent and genuine in your actions. You no longer need to hide parts of yourself or wear a mask to gain approval. Instead, you can show up fully as yourself—flaws, strengths, and all.

In your professional life, living authentically fosters trust and influence. When you act with integrity, your colleagues and superiors will recognize your reliability and value. You won't have to manipulate or pretend to succeed because your genuine efforts and true abilities will speak for themselves.

In social circles, living authentically helps you build stronger connections. You attract people who align with your values and who respect you for who you are, not for who you're pretending to be.

These authentic relationships become a source of support, inspiration, and mutual growth.

To begin living authentically in all areas of your life, ask yourself:

- What does authenticity look like for me in my personal relationships, work, and social life?
- Are there areas where I'm not being true to myself? What changes can I make to align my actions with my true values?
- How can I be more honest with myself and others in my everyday interactions?

Cultivating Respect Through Action: Leading with Empathy, Strength, and Integrity

Respect is not something you demand—it's something you earn through your actions. A true masculine leader leads by example. The strength of your leadership comes not from your position or authority, but from the integrity and empathy you demonstrate in everything you do.

Leading with Empathy:

Empathy is the ability to understand and share the feelings of others. In leadership, empathy allows you to connect with people on a deeper level. It shows that you care about their well-being, listen to their concerns, and value their perspectives. When you lead with empathy, people trust you, and they are more likely to follow your lead. Empathy builds bridges, fosters cooperation, and inspires loyalty.

Leading with Strength:

Strength is not about dominance or control. It's about having the courage to make tough decisions, stand firm in your values, and protect what you believe is right. Strength also means being resilient in the face of challenges, being able to admit when you're wrong, and constantly striving for growth. True strength is rooted in self-awareness, humility, and the ability to lift others up.

Leading with Integrity:

Integrity is doing what's right, even when no one is watching. It's about being honest, reliable, and consistent in your actions. When you lead with integrity, you build trust, and trust is the foundation of any great leader. People respect you because they know that your words align with your actions, and that your values guide every decision you make.

To cultivate respect through action, consider these steps:

- **Empathy:**

Start by listening actively to others. Practice understanding their needs, challenges, and emotions without judgment.

- **Strength:**

Be courageous in standing up for what you believe in, even if it's unpopular. Let your actions reflect your values and principles.

- **Integrity:**

Always follow through on your commitments, even when it's difficult. Be honest with yourself and others, and be willing to admit when you've made a mistake.

The Importance of Continuous Growth and Self-Improvement

True masculinity is not a destination—it's a journey. Even when you've embraced your authentic self and become a strong, respected leader, there is always room for growth. The process of self-improvement is ongoing, and it's what allows you to continue becoming the best version of yourself.

Continuous growth means always seeking new knowledge, refining your skills, and challenging your own limits. It means being open to feedback and learning from your mistakes. Self-improvement isn't just about being better at work or in your relationships—it's about becoming a more complete, balanced individual who consistently strives to grow and evolve.

To commit to continuous growth, consider:

- **Setting goals for personal development:**

    What areas of your life do you want to improve? Whether it's your emotional intelligence, your leadership skills, or your physical health, set clear goals and take actionable steps toward them.

- **Seeking feedback from others:**

    Ask trusted friends, mentors, or colleagues for honest feedback about your strengths and areas for improvement. Use their input as a tool for growth.

- **Learning from setbacks:**

   View challenges and failures as opportunities for growth, not as signs of defeat. Each setback is a chance to learn, adapt, and become better.

Remember, growth is not about perfection—it's about making progress. Every step you take toward self-improvement brings you closer to becoming the man you want to be.

Building Meaningful Relationships Based on Mutual Respect and Understanding

The quality of your relationships—whether personal, professional, or social—depends on mutual respect and understanding. As you grow in your true masculinity, you'll begin to build deeper, more meaningful connections with others. These relationships are built on trust, shared values, and empathy.

In personal relationships, being authentic and vulnerable fosters a deeper emotional bond. You will attract people who appreciate you for who you truly are and who will support you in your growth. In professional relationships, mutual respect and understanding will help you collaborate effectively, build strong teams, and inspire loyalty.

To build meaningful relationships, try:

- **Listening more than you speak:**

   Be fully present when others share their thoughts and feelings. Show them that you value their perspectives.

- **Being honest and open:**

   Share your own feelings, experiences, and challenges. Vulnerability strengthens relationships and builds trust.

- **Respecting boundaries:**

    Understand and honor the boundaries of others. Mutual respect means giving space when needed and being considerate of other people's needs.

Leaving a Legacy: How Your Actions and Leadership Shape the World Around You

The actions you take today will shape the world you leave behind. Whether you realize it or not, you are always leaving a legacy through your leadership, relationships, and choices. The legacy you leave is not defined by the material things you acquire, but by the impact you have on others and the example you set.

A true masculine leader leaves a legacy that goes beyond personal success. Your actions, integrity, and respect for others will influence the generations that come after you. When you lead with empathy, strength, and authenticity, you inspire others to do the same, creating a ripple effect of positive change.

To build a meaningful legacy:

- **Lead with intention:**

    Make sure your actions align with the values you want to pass on. Think about the kind of impact you want to have on others.

- **Inspire others to grow:**

    Your legacy is built not just on your achievements, but on how you've helped others achieve theirs. Mentor, encourage, and lift others up.

- **Live with purpose:**

    Make every decision with a sense of purpose and vision. What kind of world do you want to leave behind?

In the end, true masculinity is about living a life that is authentic, respectful, and meaningful. It's about leaving a legacy that others will remember, not because of the power you wield, but because of the way you lived, loved, and led. The world needs men who are confident in their authenticity, who lead with empathy and integrity, and who continue to grow and evolve throughout their lives. When you embrace this path, you will not only become the respected man you are meant to be—but you will also leave a lasting, positive impact on everyone around you.

Self Reflection – Chapter 4

As we've explored, living authentically and confidently in every area of your life, cultivating respect through action, and embracing continuous growth are key to embodying true masculinity. Now, it's time to translate these concepts into practical steps you can take every day. In this section, we will create a personal action plan that will guide you toward becoming the man you want to be, setting goals for your growth, and learning how to inspire others by being a role model of authenticity and respect.

1. Creating a Personal Action Plan for Embodying True Masculinity Every Day

The key to living authentically and confidently is consistency. True masculinity is not something you achieve once—it's something you embody daily. By creating a personal action plan, you'll ensure that your actions are aligned with your values and that you are consistently moving toward becoming the best version of yourself.

Here's how to create your action plan:

Step 1: Identify Your Core Values

Start by identifying the core values that define your masculinity. These are the principles that guide your decisions, relationships, and actions. Some examples might include:

- Integrity
- Authenticity
- Strength
- Empathy
- Leadership
- Respect

Once you've identified your core values, write them down and reflect on them daily. Ask yourself: How can I live in alignment with these values today?

Step 2: Define Your Daily Actions

Your action plan should include specific actions you can take each day to embody these values. For example:

- If integrity is a core value, make sure you follow through on your commitments, even in small matters.
- If empathy is important to you, practice active listening with your loved ones and colleagues.
- If strength is key, focus on developing both physical and mental resilience through exercise and self-care.

By defining your daily actions, you'll create a clear roadmap for how to live authentically each day.

Step 3: Commit to Consistency

Make a commitment to yourself to follow through on these actions each day. Consistency is the key to building trust with yourself and others. Keep track of your progress in a journal or a simple note on your phone. Reflect each week on how well you've stayed true to your values, and make adjustments as needed.

2. Setting Goals for Continued Growth and Leadership

Growth doesn't stop. In order to keep moving forward, it's important to set clear goals for your continued growth in leadership, emotional intelligence, and authenticity. These goals will help you stay on track and provide a sense of purpose and direction as you develop as a man and a leader.

Here's how to set your goals:

Step 1: Reflect on Your Current Strengths and Areas for Growth

Take a moment to assess your strengths and the areas where you could improve. Are you already living authentically in most areas of your life? Are there any specific skills, such as emotional intelligence, communication, or resilience, that you need to strengthen?

Write down your thoughts, and be honest with yourself about where you are and where you want to go.

Step 2: Set SMART Goals

Once you've identified areas for growth, set SMART goals. SMART stands for Specific, Measurable, Achievable, Relevant, and Time-bound. For example:

- **Specific:** "I will practice active listening in my relationships every day."
- **Measurable:** "I will set aside 15 minutes each day for self-reflection or journaling."
- **Achievable:** "I will read one leadership book every month to improve my leadership skills."
- **Relevant:** "I want to be a better communicator to strengthen my personal relationships."
- **Time-bound:** "By the end of the year, I want to have successfully incorporated at least three new leadership strategies into my work."

By setting SMART goals, you can track your progress and stay motivated to continue growing.

Step 3: Review and Adjust Your Goals Regularly

Growth requires flexibility. Set aside time to review your goals every few months and adjust them as necessary. If you've met a goal, celebrate your success and set a new one. If you've struggled with a goal, analyze what went wrong and adjust your strategy. Continuous reflection and adjustment are key to sustained growth.

3. Learning to Inspire Others by Being a Role Model of Authenticity and Respect

One of the most powerful ways to embrace true masculinity is by becoming a role model for others. When you live authentically and with integrity, your actions naturally inspire those around you. By consistently embodying respect, strength, and authenticity, you not only improve your own life but also positively influence the lives of others.

Here's how you can inspire others:

Step 1: Lead by Example

The most powerful way to inspire others is by leading with your actions. Show respect by listening, being honest, and following through on your commitments. Lead with strength by standing firm in your values and making decisions based on what's right, not what's easy. Lead with empathy by showing understanding and compassion to those around you.

Remember, people are watching you, whether you realize it or not. Your actions speak louder than your words.

Step 2: Share Your Journey

Being a role model doesn't mean being perfect—it means being real. Share your struggles and successes with others. Talk about the challenges you've faced in embracing your true masculinity and the lessons you've learned along the way. When you're open about your journey, you give others permission to embrace their own authenticity.

By sharing your experiences, you make it clear that growth is a lifelong process and that it's okay to struggle along the way.

Step 3: Mentor and Support Others

If you've learned valuable lessons about leadership, authenticity, and respect, consider mentoring others. Offer guidance, encouragement, and support to those who are on their own journey of personal growth. Be the example of what true masculinity looks like in action. Help others discover their own strength and authenticity by being a source of inspiration and guidance.

Conclusion

In this section, we've provided actionable insights to help you put everything you've learned into practice. By creating a personal action plan, setting goals for growth, and becoming a role model for authenticity and respect, you can continue to evolve into the confident, respected man you aspire to be.

Remember, true masculinity is not about perfection—it's about continuous growth, authenticity, and respect for yourself and others. Stay committed to your journey, and you'll not only become a better man but also inspire others to do the same. Lead with empathy, strength, and integrity, and you'll leave a lasting legacy that impacts those around you.

5

Examples of Masculine Men

Having explored the idea of true masculinity, we will now take a closer look at a few men who have lived as true embodiments of masculinity. These men did not just meet society's standards—they redefined what it means to be masculine in their own unique ways. Through their actions, mindset, and values, they became icons not because of their strength or fame, but because of the authentic masculinity they displayed.

Nelson Mandela: The Strength of Forgiveness and Leadership

Nelson Mandela is often remembered as one of the greatest leaders of the 20th century. His life was a shining example of resilience, patience, and moral courage, key elements of true masculinity. Mandela faced unimaginable suffering in the fight against apartheid, spending 27 years in prison. Yet, he never allowed bitterness or hate to define him. His true power lay in his ability to forgive and lead with compassion.

Masculine Traits:

- **Leadership**: Mandela led with wisdom, bringing people together, even those who once oppressed him, in the pursuit of a common cause. True masculinity isn't about dominance but about guiding others toward a higher purpose.

- **Resilience**: He endured years of physical and mental hardship without breaking, teaching us that masculinity isn't about avoiding suffering, but enduring it with dignity.

- **Forgiveness**: In a world that often demands revenge, Mandela chose to forgive. This takes far more strength than any battle could, and this was a defining quality of his masculinity.

Martin Luther King Jr.: Courage in the Face of Adversity

Martin Luther King Jr. is remembered for his unwavering commitment to justice and equality during the Civil Rights Movement. His message of nonviolence and equality in the face of extreme hatred and violence demonstrated the highest form of masculinity.

Masculine Traits:

- **Courage**: King spoke out against injustice, even though he knew it could cost him his life. True masculinity is about standing up for what is right, no matter the cost.

- **Integrity**: He held firm to his beliefs without compromise. Authentic masculinity is rooted in living with integrity and staying true to one's principles.

- **Selflessness**: King's mission was not for personal gain but for the betterment of society. Masculine strength often manifests in putting the needs of others before your own.

Theodore Roosevelt: Strength and Adventure in Life

Theodore Roosevelt was a man who lived life to its fullest, embodying masculine traits of adventure, vigor, and unyielding ambition. He was a war hero, a president, a writer, and a conservationist, driven by a sense of purpose and a love for life.

Masculine Traits:

- **Adventure and Boldness**: Roosevelt wasn't afraid to venture into the unknown, whether it was fighting in the Spanish-American War or exploring uncharted territories. Masculinity thrives in the willingness to take risks and embrace challenges.

- **Energy and Drive**: Roosevelt was always on the move, constantly striving to improve himself and the world around him. True masculinity involves an inner drive to accomplish, create, and lead.

- **Protectiveness**: As president, Roosevelt worked tirelessly to protect the natural beauty of America. His masculine energy was used to safeguard the things he valued most.

Steve Jobs: Visionary Leadership and Innovation

Steve Jobs revolutionized technology and business, not just because he was a brilliant innovator, but because he had a clear vision and the drive to bring it to life. His life wasn't easy, and he faced many failures along the way, but he never gave up on his mission to change the world.

Masculine Traits:

- **Vision**: Jobs saw things that others didn't. True masculinity is often about thinking beyond the present and creating something that can impact future generations.

- **Determination**: He faced setbacks, including being ousted from his own company, but he didn't let failure define him. Masculine strength comes from persistence, even when the path is hard.

- **Focus**: Jobs had an intense focus on his goals. He was known for his ability to concentrate on what mattered most and cut out distractions—an essential masculine trait.

Dwayne "The Rock" Johnson: Strength in Character and Humility

Dwayne Johnson, known as "The Rock," exemplifies modern masculinity in a powerful and relatable way. Known for his success in wrestling, acting, and business, he is admired not only for his physical strength but for his character and humility.

Masculine Traits:

- **Discipline**: Johnson's commitment to physical fitness and work ethic is remarkable. True masculinity involves a dedication to maintaining and improving oneself.

- **Humility**: Despite his fame and success, Johnson remains grounded and thankful for his journey. Humility is an often-overlooked masculine trait that fosters respect and admiration.

- **Mentorship**: The Rock often speaks about the importance of helping others along the way. Masculinity isn't about going it alone but lifting others as you rise.

Conclusion

These men—each from different walks of life—share key masculine traits that transcend time and culture. True masculinity is about living with purpose, resilience, integrity, and compassion. It's about being a leader, facing challenges head-on, and maintaining strength in the most trying of times. Whether in politics, business, or personal development, these men showed us that real masculinity isn't about domination or bravado; it's about showing up with authenticity, courage, and the unwavering belief that we are here to do something greater than ourselves.

As you look to define your own masculinity, remember that it is not about fitting a mold—it is about embracing the traits that will make you the best man you can be, one who is respected, admired, and always striving to do better.

6

My Personal Masculinity Journey

A Learning Journey About True Masculinity

As I sit down to write this chapter, I can't help but reflect on the journey I've taken to understand what true masculinity is. For many years, I was just like so many men—confused, conflicted, and searching for answers in the wrong places. I wanted to be respected, but I didn't know how to earn that respect or even what it truly meant. I followed the images of masculinity that society and the media put in front of me: tough, dominant, stoic. But deep down, something felt off. I wasn't comfortable in my own skin, and I knew that I wasn't being the man I was meant to be.

This book is not just a guide for you to find your true masculinity—it's a reflection of my own journey, the path I've walked, and the lessons I've learned along the way. It's a path from confusion to clarity, from insecurity to strength, from striving for approval to simply being confident in who I am. I hope that by sharing my personal story, you can see that you are not alone in this journey, and that it is possible to break free from the myths and misconceptions that society has placed on masculinity.

The Beginning of My Journey: Lost in the Myths of Masculinity

Like many men, I grew up surrounded by a version of masculinity that was based on stereotypes. The idea that a man had to be tough, never show emotion, and always be in control was deeply ingrained in me. This image was reinforced by the media, pop culture, and even some of the people I looked up to—whether it was the action movie heroes, athletes, or even some of the men in my own family. I was taught that to be respected, I had to be dominant, stoic, and emotionally distant.

At first, I tried to embody these ideals. I thought that showing emotions made me weak, that being vulnerable would make others lose respect for me. I kept my feelings bottled up, convinced that I had to be the "tough guy" in all aspects of my life. But no matter how hard I tried, something inside me didn't feel right. I wasn't truly happy, and I certainly wasn't as respected as I thought I should be.

The turning point came when I realized that I was constantly suppressing who I truly was. The more I tried to live up to society's distorted version of masculinity, the more conflicted I became. I was living in a way that didn't align with my true self, and this created a lot of inner tension. The confusion I felt was overwhelming, but it was also a wake-up call. I knew I had to change, but I wasn't sure how.

Rebuilding Masculinity: Discovering True Strength, Integrity, and Authenticity

The process of redefining masculinity for myself began with a simple realization: True masculinity isn't about fitting into a mold or living up to someone else's expectations. It's about strength, integrity, and authenticity—qualities that come from within, not from external pressures.

One of the first things I had to do was get clear about who I was. I began reflecting on my values, what I truly stood for, and what kind of man I wanted to be. I realized that strength wasn't about being physically tough or emotionally closed off. It was about the courage to be vulnerable and the strength to face my own fears. Integrity wasn't just about doing the right thing when people were watching—it was about living in alignment with my values, even when no one else knew.

I also learned that authenticity was the foundation of it all. Trying to be someone I wasn't had only created confusion and dissatisfaction in my life. When I started to embrace my true self, flaws and all, I felt a sense of freedom and peace that I had never experienced before. I stopped trying to be the "perfect man" that society demanded, and instead, I focused on being the best version of myself. I learned to accept that it's okay to be imperfect and that true masculinity is about embracing who I am, rather than pretending to be something I'm not.

Embracing Emotions and Vulnerability: The Road to Confidence

For me, one of the hardest parts of this journey was learning to embrace my emotions. Growing up, I had been taught that emotions were something to hide, especially the "weak" ones like fear or sadness. But as I began to grow and learn more about true masculinity, I realized that emotions are not a sign of weakness. They are a part of being human.

I had to start allowing myself to feel, to express my emotions without judgment. It wasn't easy, and at first, it felt uncomfortable. But slowly, I began to realize that embracing vulnerability was not only empowering—it was necessary. Vulnerability is a source of strength because it allows you to connect with others on a deeper level. It allows you to lead with empathy, to listen and understand, and to truly inspire others by showing them that it's okay to be imperfect.

As I embraced vulnerability, my relationships began to improve. I was able to communicate more openly with my loved ones, and I found that I was able to build stronger, more meaningful connections. I started to show up as my authentic self—emotionally, mentally, and physically. And through this, I gained a sense of confidence that wasn't based on arrogance or dominance, but on self-awareness and self-acceptance.

Becoming a Leader: Leading by Example, Not by Force

One of the most profound shifts in my journey came when I realized that true leadership comes not from asserting dominance, but from inspiring respect through actions. I used to think that being a leader meant always having control, always having the answers, and never showing any weakness. But true leadership is about leading with empathy, strength, and integrity. It's about being a role model, not because you demand respect, but because you earn it through your actions.

I started focusing on leading by example. I stopped trying to control everything and instead started empowering those around me. I learned that leadership isn't about being the loudest voice in the room—it's about listening, understanding, and acting with integrity. I began to inspire respect not by asserting my power over others, but by leading with authenticity and showing up with strength, even in vulnerable moments.

Leaving a Legacy: The Impact of True Masculinity

As I look back on my journey, I realize that embracing true masculinity has not only transformed my own life, but it's also allowed me to make a positive impact on those around me. I've learned that the true measure of a man is not in the power he holds, but in the way he treats others and the legacy he leaves behind.

The man I am today is not perfect, but he is real. He is strong, authentic, and committed to continuous growth. I have learned that masculinity is not something to be feared or suppressed—it is something to be embraced fully, in all its forms. True masculinity is about living with integrity, leading with respect, and connecting with others from a place of authenticity and vulnerability.

This journey hasn't been easy, and there have been many times I've had to confront my own doubts and insecurities. But every step I've taken has led me closer to becoming the man I am meant to be. I am proud of who

I've become, and I know that this journey of growth will continue. And my hope is that by sharing my story, you too will be inspired to embrace your true masculinity and step into the confident, respected man you are meant to be.

The journey from confusion to clarity, from insecurity to strength, is a path that every man must walk in his own way. But I promise you, the destination is worth it. When you embrace your authentic self and live with integrity, you will not only transform your own life—you will inspire others to do the same. And that, in itself, is a legacy worth leaving.

Conclusion

As we come to the end of this journey together, I want to leave you with a simple but powerful truth: True masculinity isn't about fitting into a mold or meeting society's expectations. It's about embracing your authentic self, living with integrity, and leading with strength and respect.

Throughout this book, we've explored the myths and misconceptions about masculinity that have been ingrained in us by media, culture, and social pressures. We've broken down those stereotypes and looked at what it really means to be a man. We've talked about the importance of self-awareness, embracing vulnerability, and overcoming fear. We've also discussed how to lead with authenticity and respect, and how to build meaningful relationships based on these values.

But most importantly, we've focused on helping you make the shift from confusion to clarity—from living under the weight of society's distorted image of masculinity to embracing the strength and power that come from being your true, authentic self.

I want you to understand that this journey is not something that happens overnight. It's a lifelong process. Each day is an opportunity to align your actions with your values, to step into your full potential, and to inspire those around you. There will be challenges along the way—times when you doubt yourself or when society pushes you to conform. But with every challenge, there is an opportunity for growth.

As you move forward, remember this: True masculinity is not about perfection, it's about authenticity. It's about being strong enough to show vulnerability, confident enough to live by your values, and humble enough to lead by example. When you lead with integrity, respect, and empathy, you will earn the respect of others—not because of your power or dominance, but because of the strength of your character.

So, as you take the lessons from this book and apply them to your life, don't focus on being "perfect." Instead, focus on becoming the best version of yourself. Embrace your authenticity, continue to grow, and lead by the example of respect and strength. You are capable of far more than you know, and the world is waiting for you to step into your full potential.

In the end, this journey isn't just about you. It's about the legacy you'll leave, the positive impact you'll make on those around you, and the example you'll set for future generations of men. When you embrace your true masculinity, you not only transform your own life, but you also inspire others to do the same.

Thank you for taking this journey with me. I believe in your ability to become the respected man you are meant to be. Keep moving forward with confidence, authenticity, and strength.

References

Listed below are a number of references used to write this book as well as my personal experience.

1. Howes, L. (2017). *The Mask of Masculinity: How Men Can Embrace Vulnerability, Create Strong Relationships, and Live Their Fullest Lives.* Harmony Books.

   This book explores the societal pressures and stereotypes surrounding modern masculinity, offering a path for men to break free from these limiting views and embrace a more authentic, emotionally fulfilling life.

2. Deida, D. (2006). *The Way of the Superior Man: A Spiritual Guide to Mastering the Challenges of Women, Work, and Sexual Desire.* Sounds True. Deida discusses the deeper aspects of masculinity, urging men to balance strength, vulnerability, and authenticity in their relationships and personal growth.

3. Frankl, V. E. (2006). *Man's Search for Meaning.* Beacon Press. Frankl's exploration of his experiences in Nazi concentration camps provides profound insights into how men can find purpose and strength, emphasizing personal responsibility and meaning over external expectations.

4. Brown, B. (2015). *Rising Strong: The Reckoning. The Rumble. The Revolution.* Random House.

   Brown examines how embracing vulnerability and facing emotional struggles head-on can lead to growth and resilience, focusing on how men can become stronger through emotional honesty.

5. Eldredge, J. (2001). *Wild at Heart: Discovering the Secret of a Man's Soul.* Thomas Nelson.

   Eldredge explores the call to adventure and emotional authenticity for men, encouraging them to embrace their masculinity in a way that reflects strength and personal growth.

6. Glover, R. A. (2003). *No More Mr. Nice Guy: A Proven Plan for Getting What You Want in Love, Sex, and Life.* Running Press.

   Glover's book addresses how many men suppress their desires and avoid conflict in the name of being "nice," helping them reconnect with their authenticity and gain more control over their lives.

7. Brown, B. (2012). *Daring Greatly: How the Courage to Be Vulnerable Transforms the Way We Live, Love, Parent, and Lead.* Gotham Books.

   Brown expands on the concept of vulnerability as a strength, encouraging men to embrace authenticity and emotional honesty to lead fulfilling lives and relationships.

8. *The Art of Manliness* (n.d.). Retrieved from https://www.artofmanliness.com

    This comprehensive website offers articles, podcasts, and guides on various aspects of masculinity, from personal growth and emotional intelligence to leadership and self-discipline, helping men live balanced, authentic lives.

9. Biddulph, S. (2010). *The New Manhood: The 10 Essential Experiences Every Man Should Have.* Finch Publishing.

    Biddulph challenges traditional views of masculinity and explores how men can redefine themselves in ways that lead to greater happiness, self-respect, and meaningful connections.

www.ingramcontent.com/pod-product-compliance
Lightning Source LLC
Chambersburg PA
CBHW030516130626
46549CB00007B/3016